I'm with Shea

By

Shea Kayla Shawhan

Dedication

I want to dedicate this book to Touché.

This book is for my sweet puppy, once you left me my whole world came crashing down on me and I totally lost my mind. I was so sad and mad at the same time when I heard you had died, mainly because I wasn't there for you as I would have liked to have been.

You, my little brown doxie, have a special spot in my heart that has left a permanent mark on me that has been forever embedded. You were my sunshine on a rainy day and could always put a smile to my face, but I hope you, my sweetheart of a dog, are hopefully running through a patch of grass and flowers and loving your little life on the other side because I sure loved you and will forever love you. I hope one day that when I get there with you that you could help that same smile return to me. Until then my dear little one, I hope you continue to run through those flower fields and I want you to know how much mama loves you.

Table of Contents

Chapter 1: Trials and tribulations!

Chapter 2: Learning into a pole.

Chapter 3: Pups! There it is.

Chapter 4: Blue

Chapter 5: Is it naptime already?

Chapter 6: Half Field

Chapter 7: Diamonds are a girl's best friend.

Chapter 8: Tee-peed

Chapter 9: A pretty penny

Chapter 10: Bubbles and Buttercup

Chapter 11: For Sale

Chapter 12: Girls just want to have fun.

Chapter 13: Sprinkler mishaps

Chapter 14: You're in Trouble

Chapter 15: Trolls Exist?

Chapter 16: Olive Fingers?

Chapter 17: Stomping Spiders!

Chapter 18: Grass skirts and a Hawaiian roller coaster ride

Chapter 19: leprechauns and four-leaf clovers

Chapter 20: Bickerton

Chapter 21: Four wheelin'

Chapter 22: Sache, TX

Chapter 23: Wienerschnitzel games

Chapter 24: Rock Solid

Chapter 25: If I went mad, we must have a cup of tea.

Chapter 26: Peeps and Runways

Chapter 27: Help I've Fallen and can't get up.

Chapter 28: Ride or Die

Chapter 29: Gadgets and gizmos a – plenty

Chapter 30: I'm With Shea

Chapter 31: Graduation

Chapter 32: Parade of Colors

Chapter 33: Home Sweet home

Chapter 34: Falling into boxes.

Chapter 35: Kitties R. US

Chapter 36: Courts in Session

Chapter 37: Saddle up!

Chapter 38: And the parade of colors continues.

Chapter 39: Palm trees, a cool breeze and a "Yes, please"

Chapter 40: Trouble in Paradise

Chapter 41: Rehab for one

Chapter 42: This beauty is a beast.

Chapter 43: Salon a la' mode

Chapter 44: The day Touché found her wings!

Chapter 45: Let's just have one more seizure, shall we?

Chapter 46: Bruised but not broken

Chapter47: Where the green grass grows

Chapter 48: Love is an open door

Chapter 49: Did someone order an ice cream?

Chapter 50: Ooh Rah

Chapter 51: Faith, Trust and Pixie Dust

Chapter 52: Get your booty and shine your doubloons, this is gonna be one tough sea.

Chapter 53: Fins up

Chapter 54: Halos glowing tonight!

Chapter 55: Back in the Sunshine State

Chapter 1: Fun in the sun!

My name is Shea, and this is my story.

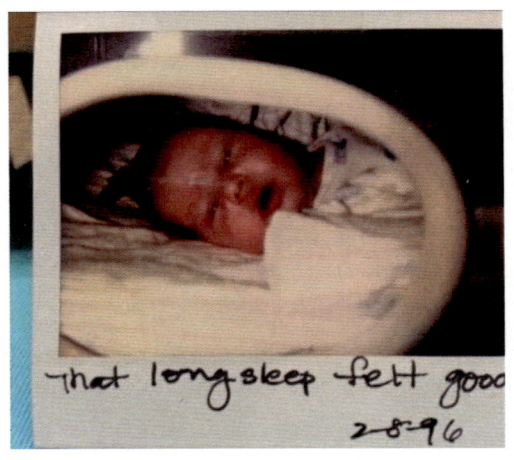

First let's start when I was born January 30th, 1996, in Newport Beach, California. I was born at Hoag hospital. I was 8 lbs. 6oz and 22 inches. My dad was deployed overseas and had to get permission to go on leave. Well, my doctor tried to do a normal birth, but my head kept hitting mom's cervix repeatedly and then when I finally came out, I was seizing and had to go straight into the NICU until they stopped.

I was placed into a coma to let my brain injury calm down from the traumatic birth. Finally, I was okay, and that long sleep felt good on 2-8-1996.

My mom then got thyroid cancer for some time and after a while she beat it. We lived with my grandparents at the time in California. I was two years old at the time when my parents made the decision to move to Virgina where we had a basset hound.

Well soon they got a divorce. After that my mom and I moved back to California to be with my grandparents so they could help raise me.

Chapter 2: Learning into a pole.

Soon I got put into an early learning center called TLC. One day we went out of our classroom and our teacher put us all in a line and we started walking.

Well, if you know me you know I'm a klutz; and if you don't, well, welcome. I remember my teacher lining us up and we started walking out of the class and I remember all the other kids where straight in line. Well not this girl. I was the one twirling around and not paying any attention whatsoever and then wham!

My face hit a pole. Well, I look up and I see this big pole while I regain where I am for a bit before jumping back in line. I think my teacher heard and looked to see what happened and I just smiled.

Well, at my learning center I was also enrolled in tap dance lessons. I had my black leotard and bright sparkly pink skirt which had a button on it and had Disney princesses on it, which were Ariel, Cinderella, Belle and Snow White.

By our front door was a small thing of tile and I got in my outfit and told everyone to gather by the front so I could show them what I could do, and I tapped my little heart out.

Chapter 3: Pups, there it is!

Soon it was Christmas and everyone gathered around the living room in front of the tree one by one. It was seven o' clock in the morning with everyone still in their pajamas and sitting on the couch. Before I even touched presents, there were cameras ready to capture the memory and then as they started rolling the recording, one by one I started unwrapping presents throwing wrapping paper over my head and loving every moment of it.

After a while and a few presents, my mom starts to get off the couch to help my aunt inside. I was so excited to see her. As I turn around to give her a hug I suddenly see a tiny dark brown dachshund in her arms with a hot pink bow around her neck and a white tag that read "To: Shea."

I instantly fell in love with her and forgot all about the other presents. But as I put her on the floor to finish opening the rest of my presents, she ran around with her pink bow getting in the way of her tiny paws then she got picked up to be on the couch and I tried rushing through every present to play with my new puppy. Finally, after all the presents were opened, all I wanted was to play with Touché. Her ears bounced up and down as she ran as I threw a ball.

24/7 that's all she wanted to do. Over time she started getting bigger until she was full grown, and I fell in love with her even more. She became very spoiled, had everything handed to her and was loved on every day. I was a very proud dachshund mama.

Chapter 4: Blue

As a little girl my favorite show was Blue's Clues. It would come on and it would be my lunchtime show and my grandma would cook me beans and franks for my lunch, and I would sit down a happy girl and be content.

On the TV, they said, "Where's blue?" And I would scream at the TV, "She's right there!" Then the man on the TV went over and there was a paw print, and he got a paper out with his crayon and drew the object. As soon as he got all three clues he went back to his chair, sat down, and started to piece all three clues together onto what blue wanted to do.

After he pieced all the clues together, he said, "You helped me figure out all the clues."

It was a very short show every time, but I loved it.

Chapter 5: Is it naptime already?

Well every night at bedtime my grandpa would read me a book. I got my teeth brushed, picked out a book to read and jumped into bed. My grandpa covered me up with the bed covers sat down and opened the book to start reading to me. I loved this time with him and we would laugh and smile while he was reading to me.

After a couple of pages, he was asleep, eyes closed, and he was out like a light while he left me hanging in the middle of the book. Well then I looked up and saw him asleep and I shook him awake and said, "It's not over or naptime right now. It's story time." He continued to read on. Then he got a few more pages in and again fell asleep; and again I shook him awake and said, "Grandpa, the story." He just looked at me, smiled, and said, "Oh, I thought it was my naptime."

I said, "Not until I finish my book and then it's grandpa's turn to take a nap." Then he finished the book, tucked me back in all warm and snuggly and turned around and put on my Disney princess lullaby CD and kissed me goodnight on my forehead and said he loves me and shut my door and I turned over and fell fast asleep.

Chapter 6: Half Field

Soon I got into sports, and I started with soccer. I enjoyed it so much. Our colors were purple, and we were called the 'Purple People Eaters' and, no, we did not eat people.

I had a game one afternoon and was ready to go. As we jumped into the car to leave, I was bouncing from excitement. Once we got there, we saw my coach and some cones. We got out of the car and started to walk up to the grass. I put my ball down and started working on some passes on the side while waiting for everyone else to show. I started passing the ball to a family member so I could get warmed up and soon more girls started to show. So we started on the drills we saw laid out for us-in and out and if we touched a cone, you went back into the back of the line.

Soon, the game that was playing before us was all done and I bent down to grab my ball and started walking with my team. As soon as we got to the field we had some time before the game started so I went to the sidelines where my mom was standing and drank some water out of my water bottle and then went onto the field and the game began.

I was running back and forth soon I saw this girl with the ball; mind you she was bigger than me and that was when I thought I was creamed for sure but somehow an ounce of courage in me wanted to show up that day and I ran towards her and swiped the ball then at the corner of my eye I saw two girls from the other team coming up behind me but I made it to half field and stepped back and kicked the ball. It went over the girls' heads and into the net. Goal!

All I could hear was the crowd roaring and I ran to the sidelines I couldn't believe it. I scored the winning goal. I ran over to the sidelines where my mom was and gave her a hug and said, "Did you see that?" and we all celebrated that day and went back home.

Chapter 7: Diamonds are a girl's best friend.

Soon, I got tired of soccer and wanted a change, so I decided to jump into softball. I got into softball because my mom played at Golden West High School in California. Her number was 12 so I decided that was going to be my number as well. I even got her old softball bag that had her last name on it (Byrd) and to the side it said number 12. I cherished that bag.

Soon we started our warm-ups as soon as some other girls showed up. My mom and my grandma were the coaches and after a couple drills and throws. As soon as it was time we started heading to the dirt field.

I was really excited and wanted to make my mom really proud; well we had our batting line up in order and I was the third batter up. I thought it was because I was her kid. I came up to the plate, lined myself up, twirled my bat, set my feet and waited for my pitch. The pitcher wound up and threw the first pitch: ball one. I stepped out of the box and took a couple of practice swings. As I got back in the box and saw her do her wind up; the ball left her fingertips and I saw it go by: strike one. Now I got a feel for her; at the next pitch I drove it to left field. I saw that ball skyrocket to the fence and got a double out of it. Well we had one on base with one out and one up to bat. Before I knew it, we suddenly had two outs and I was praying that one of my teammates could help me move bases.

    I got my prayer answered. She came up to bat, and on the first pitch, foul ball. But on the second pitch crushed it into centerfield and I ran home and now it was 1-0 with a girl on second and two outs. We were ahead but not by much and I was hopeful because my next teammate up looked good. She went up to base and first pitch she saw ripped one to left field. It dropped and she got a single. We screamed and chanted. We were still alive and had the next girl moving to home plate. I could tell she was nervous. First pitch, strike; then the second, a ball. On the third pitch, a pop up fly ball. and she was out.

Well now it was time to take the field. I was put at first base just like my mom was, and ready for anything to come my way. The first batter was up and I took a breath and said "play ball" in my head. First pitch, a ball; second pitch, strike; and when the umpire is saying these was yelling em' right in your ear, it made your ear ring for a while.

Well it was three up, three down with two girls on bases. And our turn to bat again. Well we didn't have much luck either until the middle of the innings and had our breakthrough moment. Finally it was the middle of one of the innings and we had bases loaded with only one out and I was up to bat again. I looked over to see my mom coaching by third base and she just whispered, "crush it." I planted my feet in the box, took a breath and on the first pitch crushed it. Home Run!

I couldn't believe it. I drug in the three runs and came in making it 5-0 and I looked over my shoulder after returning to home plate to see my mom and she just smiled. Well soon the other team was mad and I could tell and soon we had our three outs and the other team was up to bat and this was our downfall.

I think it was because we were getting tired and the sun came out and was beating down on our backs so we gave up three runs just like that. Now it was 3-5 and soon it was the last inning and I was sweating. Another girl up to bat with two outs; one more out and we won. She got up to the box and crushed it but our left field caught the ball and we won the game. We threw our gloves down and ran to each other and cheered that night.

Chapter 8: Tee-peed

I stayed in contact with my softball team after the season was over and my mom and grandma came up with the idea that we should have a sleepover at our house that night. I was excited; we were going to have karaoke, snacks, and Kool aid. Well, we heard the doorbell go off and soon every girl was over, and we officially started the sleepover. We rolled out all our sleeping bags on the carpet in our living room and started getting everything set up for that night.

Then we got straight into the night with a couple songs and I sang "Soak up the sun" by Sheryl Crow. We had a blast, everyone singing and laughing along, but like all good times it had to come to an end and we got settled into our sleeping bags for the night. But then my mom woke us up and said we should grab some toilet paper and follow her outside.

We got out of our bags we were in and grabbed rolls and followed her. Once we were outside in front of my house she said who wants to toilet paper the neighbor's house. We all looked at each other and said, "Oh yeah." So we took our toilet paper went across the street to our neighbor's house and started throwing toilet paper on their roof, bushes and even their lawn. As we saw a light turn on, everyone scattered and ran back to my house and fell back asleep.

Well, the next morning we all woke up and went outside and saw my house toilet papered everything was covered as well and we all had to clean it back up. I just want to say it took a long time, but it was so fun and worth every roll we threw. Soon the sleepover ended, and parents started picking up everyone and we gave hugs and said best sleepover ever!

Chapter 9: A Pretty Penny

As a little girl growing up, believe it or not, I got into trouble. I don't remember being a little rebel but apparently my grandpa does and he says he remembers my not so great moments. Maybe I just wanted to block those memories out of my mind. LOL. He said I would get on his nerves and then he would tell me, "You know, I could sell you to the gypsies and get myself a pretty penny off of you." I just looked at him and said, "You wouldn't dare sell me; I'm your buddy." He smiled and said, "Yes you are.

But they are looking for a little girl just like you and all I have to do is pick up the phone and call 1-800 gypsies and they would be over." Well I got so scared and clung onto his arm and said, "No, don't let them take me grandpa. I don't want to leave. I'll be good, I promise." To this day my grandpa uses that even to my dog. I just figured it was his phrase. My dog didn't believe him though, and looked at him and laid her head back down and closed her eyes again. And I see that even Touché's not scared of the gypsies and continued playing with my toys.

Chapter 10: Bubbles and Buttercup

As I grew, I was watching a TV show called "The Powder Puff girls, an American superhero animated television show series. The show centered on three kindergarten-aged girls with superpowers named Blossom, Buttercup and Bubbles. They lived in the fictional city of Townsville with their dad and creator. The three girls were called upon by the city's mayor to help fight nearby criminals and other enemies using their powers.

Well, then I had an idea and ran to my grandparents and said, "Is it okay if I can have a pet fish. I finally got my grandpa to say "sure" and we jumped in his van and headed to the pet shop. As we arrived and got out, we walked up to the door and started looking around. We started in the front of the shop and worked our way back of the store where the fish were. I saw them in tanks swimming around I saw these two fish and I tapped on my grandpa's shoulder and I pointed to one tank and it had a couple fish in it. I looked at these two fish and said, "I like these," and they listed out the pricing for them. They also listed out the accessories and I looked at my grandpa and he said, "Anything for my little princess."

I smiled, gave him a hug and we bought everything and walked out of the pet store and drove back home.

As we got home, we grabbed the new fish tank we bought and decorated it and filled it up with water; my grandpa asked me what I was going to name my fish and I looked down at both and looked back up and said I think we should name them Bubbles and Buttercup. Soon he got the fish that the shop put in little baggies for both fish filled up with water and cut the bags open and poured both tiny fish into the tank and we set the tank inside by the front door.

Chapter 11: For Sale

Growing up I only had two friends in the neighborhood but hung out with all the neighbors.

I was playing outside and riding my bike around and having a good time and wasn't looking where I was again like I normally do. Then all you could hear is this loud smack and I fell off my bike and it was like seeing stars above my head spinning around. I got up and there were drops of blood coming down and a big lump where I hit my head. My friend, Annalee, started yelling for my grandma to come out and help me. As she exited the house and shut the door, she saw me with drops of blood running down my face and went back inside grabbed a plastic bag filled with some ice and came back out. She walked across the street and handed me the bag to put on my head and I put it on and she said, "I think that is enough riding around for today," and she took my hand and we walked back over and walked in our house. Everyone gathered around me like a swarm of bees trying to get honey and asked what happened. I said I bumped my head on the for-sale sign at the neighbor's house and for the rest of the day I was on rest mode until my head felt a little better.

Chapter 12: Girls just wanna have fun!

A few days after and I was starting to feel better I was on the couch watching TV with Touché when I heard the doorbell ring. I got up and Touché followed suit and went down the ramp my grandpa made for her so she doesn't hurt her back. I opened the door. It was my friends Anna and Mariah and they wanted to play.

I was excited to see my friends and let them inside and we had the idea of playing dress up. We all ran past the living room and opened the glass sliding door to open another room and we started pretending to play hair salon and getting dressed up in all of my princess dresses I had. I sat down and they started to brush my hair and blow dry it out. We all took turns playing hair salon and when everyone had their turn, we all went to go show my family how pretty we were as we acted like we were on the runway walking down while everyone said, "Oh look how gorgeous the girls are."

We pretended we were going down a runway. Then as soon as we got done showing everyone, the girls had to go back home and so we went back to take off the dresses and the hair accessories and we hugged goodbye and walked them back out and then I came back home to snuggle with my puppy again.

Chapter 13: Sprinkler Mishaps

It was a hot day in Huntington Beach CA, and we were sweating so I asked my grandpa if we could bring out the sprinkler and jump through it my friends were outside and I invited them over to jump in the sprinkler with me since it was so hot outside. All three of us were in my front lawn jumping into the sprinkler; it was so refreshing when the water touched my skin.

All three of us were really enjoying ourselves and having fun and laughing and then when I jumped over the sprinkler one time out of all the other jumps, as I jumped I hit my toe on the sprinkler - of course; right, did I mention I'm a klutz. Well, then I looked at my toe and I saw the blood immediately and stopped and sat down and got a band-aid and wrapped it around my toe; and then we could say we were all done with the sprinkler. I got up to hug my friends and they went back home and also so they could get into another pair of clothes and out of their bathing suits. My grandparents took me back inside; I went into my room and grabbed my little mermaid bath toys while my grandpa was filling up the tub for my bath.

He said to stop it halfway and left and went back downstairs. I stopped the water and started playing for a whole 45 minutes maybe and played with my little mermaid figurines; then got out, dried myself off and put on my pjs and went downstairs.

Chapter 14: You're in Trouble

My grandpa was laying on the carpet watching TV and I asked him if he was up to a game of Trouble. He said, "Sure if you want me to beat you;" and I replied with, "Not a chance." We laughed and said let's see what you got. We started to get the board game out and setting our colors out and started popping away.

Well, it went back and forth for a long time both of us landing on each other's pegs until I started to go on a roll and kept popping the dice and landing on the high numbers and my grandpa would say, "Darlene, make her stop!" My grandma would just say, "She's good;" and just like that I beat him. I asked if he wanted to play again, and he said best two out of three. We played with ending it as a tie and us coming to an agreement and having a fun night that night.

Chapter 15: Trolls Exist?

    Well, it was another pretty day in Huntington Beach, California. My grandpa asked me after lunch if I wanted to take a bike ride with him down to the bird sanctuary and I said, "Yes, I would love that." Soon it was lunch time for Shea-Shea and my grandma made me a kid cuisine which had chicken nuggets, mac and cheese, corn and for dessert chocolate pudding with star sprinkles mixed in. I got a TV tray and sat everything down with my little Sunny D drink while watching - yes - Blues Clues.

    After I ate everything and I got up to throw everything away and handed my grandma my spoon back, I said thank you and started to head into the garage with my grandpa to get our bikes and put helmets on and started to ride down to the sanctuary. After riding for a while we arrived and went down the dirt road and then when we got closer there was a bike path and water where we let go of my fish.

    We rode it down until we hit a bridge and as soon as we got closer he said to turn onto the bridge. I said okay cause we had to go to the other side to see all the creatures I wanted to see that day so I turned and we were on the bridge and he said the evil trolls would come out and say you had to pay a toll for going across the bridge.

If not, they would eat me if I didn't pay and I remember getting off my bike and looking down to see if anyone was there then getting back on my bike and going across.

We saw a fox that day and snakes as we were riding and pelicans diving for fish then there was this one big hill and we went up; but then I started to go downhill on my bike and scared my grandpa half to death and then after getting my balance and footing back I started to go back up the hill to continue our journey.

Chapter 16: Olive Fingers?

As soon as we got back from the bird sanctuary, we put our bikes back and my grandma was in the kitchen cooking dinner and in a separate tiny bowl were black olives, my favorite. Well for dinner my grandma made brisket, mashed potatoes, corn, and I had my olives for me. Well, I grabbed a couple olives and then I held out my hand and I put the olives on my fingers and I was so pleased with myself and showed my family and then I laughed and ate the olives off of my fingers. I got that from my grandpa's side of the family.

I always thought of myself as a special little thing and I guess it was true. After dinner was over I asked if there were any more olives left cause I told my grandma I missed my olive fingers and she said she could put a few more back in the bowl for me. I gave her a hug and went back to the table, and she put the bowl back down and I started again putting the olives back on my fingers being just being one happy little girl.

Chapter 17: Stomping Spiders!

The next day my grandpa and I went to the park; we took our bikes again and in the parking lot were concreate stop blocks. We would weave our bikes through them before going up and through the basketball courts and fences to the playground where the swings and everything else were. Once we got to the playground we jumped off our bikes and I went onto the playground. We played my favorite game as a kid, Stomping Spiders, which was I would go on the flat surface on the playground and I remember it had little holes or slots.

My grandpa would find a stick pick it up and poke it through the hole and it would be a "Spider" and I would stomp on the stick before my grandpa would quickly try to remove it before I could stomp on it. With some he was really quick and some I stomped on it. We kept playing until we saw it was getting late or as well we stopped when we started getting tired and headed back to the house so he could sit on the couch and relax for a while and I played with Touché as soon as we got home.

Chapter 18: Grass Skirts and a Hawaiian Roller Coaster Ride

I had another childhood friend; her name was Danielle. We lived four doors down from her, and she was having her birthday party and invited me. The invitation said come have an epic Hawaiian roller coaster of a time with Danielle and luau the night away.

And make sure to bring or wear your grass skirts. I wore mine down and started to walk to her house. Once I got there I knocked on her door and waited for the door to be opened. Once someone came to the door they saw me and smiled and said, "Shea, welcome, Danielle is in the next room. As I made my way in their house and to where my friend was, I saw a CD player and a CD that had Lilo and Stitch music on it. Once everyone arrived the party began and we hula'd and our grass skirts swayed to the rhythm. We were at her party for an hour before it shut down and everyone started to return home or get picked up. I was the last one to leave and I gave her a hug and said that I enjoyed her party and I would play with her again another day. Then I thanked her dad and walked out the door and started to walk back to my house.

Chapter 19: Leprechauns and four-leaf Clovers

Well, I know I haven't talked about my schooling much besides my TLC years but here you go another chapter on my schooling. I was in the first grade when St. Patrick's Day came around and was not wearing any green that day. Well I was driven to my school and was walked in by my grandma. I hugged her bye and entered my classroom for the day. We all had our own spot and color on the rug. My color was purple – coincidence? I think not! My favorite color! I sat down and class started; I listened to the teacher for a while before we left the class to go play on the playground.

While we were walking all of a sudden I felt a pinch on my shoulder. I looked around and no one was there. I rubbed my shoulder and soon we were about to go back to the class. Once we got back all of the desks were painted green and had four leaf clovers on our desks. We hunted to see who had come into our class while we were gone and the teacher said, "Oh no, he has come and this is his warning. He wants his pot of gold and he wants it now!"

We all stared at each other and said that we don't have any gold and then we got pinched again. The day ended and as we were going home, I explained my day to my mom in the best way possible and she said that it sounded interesting as we were driving back home.

Chapter 20: Bickerton

Growing up, my grandpa played softball and his softball name was Bickerton and I would go watch him play. I loved watching him while he was up to bat. I would scream, "Grandpa, hit a home run for me," as he played. I went to every game with my grandparents. I got more excited watching him play.

But yes, the sun was hot, and I got tired over time throughout the game. I had a tent I could go into and take a nap and had my snacks while the game was proceeding to play and then after a while I would wake up and see the game almost over. My grandpa even told me that was when I learned very colorful language because of all the men around and - I'm guessing here - used it when they struck out. And as soon as the games ended, I would always run back to grampa and jump into his arms and give him a huge hug and said, "Good job, grandpa."

Chapter 21: Four Wheelin'

Well, we soon moved from California to Centerfield, Texas. I came here to live with my uncle and aunt and cousin in their trailer. I was living the country life running outside with my cousin, playing, catching this and that which probably shouldn't have been caught and watching all the butterflies fly about and played with all the dogs that was running around.

As I was growing up with them, I had my own room and loved living with them. My uncle was a police officer at the time and was often radioed in on the job time-to-time and had to go to work.

Well we also had a four wheeler and my cousin and I decided we wanted to go for a ride that night, so we headed out of the trailer and down the stairs to the four wheeler and got on. I was the passenger while my cousin drove. After going around the trailer a couple times I wanted a turn at driving us around so we swapped place. Well I was starting to move and before I was even at the time to turn my cousin was screaming "turn turn turn" so I listened to her and turned the wheel and the four wheeler ran into the trailer.

Half my body was underneath the trailer and my cousin started screaming for my mom and her mom to come out and as they opened the door and started down the stairs to us my mom saw me with half of my body underneath the trailer and said, "How did this happen?"

We kind of shrugged our shoulders and then my uncle came out as well and saw his niece under his trailer and he said okay were gonna have to pull you until you're back out. They pulled and pulled and pulled and finally I came out and was crying. All I wanted was to go back into the trailer and sit and relax for the rest of the night and that's what we did but would soon find out there was going to be a surprise around the corner.

Chapter 22: Sachse, Tx

We were still in Texas but only moved to a different state after my aunt and uncle got a divorce. We moved to a city called Sache, Texas. Remember that surprise? Yep, my aunt was pregnant again and I was going to have another cousin coming our way.

I did some of my more schooling here as well and we had a tiny apartment and four people lived here. So in this chapter let's start at school, shall we? I was just getting out of school and coming home. As the bus dropped me off, I entered the apartment and set my backpack down and I went to the restroom before starting my homework that night.

I came out, unzipped my bag, and took out my binder with my homework. As I just barely started it, my aunt comes in the room and welcomes me home and gives me a hug. A few moments later she tells me that she was going to the mailbox to get the mail and she would be back and told me what time.

I said okay and resumed my homework. As she walked out the door I was writing when I looked at the clock and saw it was the time she said she would be back and wasn't. So I panicked and stopped doing my homework, opened our back door and walked out and started walking towards the mailboxes.

I saw she wasn't there; so what did I do? I started walking down the highway yelling for my aunt and wondering where she went. Well, as I was on the highway, she was back home and entered the apartment and saw I wasn't there with the back door wide open and got scared and called the cops.

They came to the house and immediately went to find me. As soon as one officer found me, they brought me back home and said she's safe. Once I entered the apartment I finished my homework for the night.

Pretty soon it was time for my aunt to go into labor and she had my cousin, a baby girl named Logan. She stayed in the hospital for a bit before they allowed her to come home. As soon as she left the hospital, and we arrived back at the apartment, we relaxed for the night.

Soon Rachael wanted a dog and begged my aunt if she could have a dog. She agreed to it and bought her a dachshund named Abby. She was a dapple and had one brown eye and one blue eye. One day we left for the afternoon and left Abby alone in the apartment. When we came back, we saw the blinds torn up and were all a mess.

My aunt called my grandparents and asked if they could take Abby and bring her back with them to California. Abby soon became a Cali dog, and my grandparents wanted Touché to have another friend to play with.

Chapter 23: Wienerschnitzel Races

We went to California and brought little Abby with us and, man oh man, did she become a Cali dog in a heartbeat. Bathing in the sun, long walks around the block and so on. She soon became full grown and the second cutest dachshund in California. The first was my girl Touché.

One day we saw on TV races for German wiener dogs. We looked at each other, and we signed both of our girls up right away. There were so many dachshunds. Well, we got to a table and sat down. While we were waiting, I put on Touché's costume - a hot dog with mustard stripes on it. Both of us started practicing with our girls. Soon we heard over the intercom it was time to start the race. I took off her costume, and we started to line our pups at the starting line. They counted down and Abby took off but it took Touché a while but once she saw me and I patted my legs for her to come, there she went like a princess down the track.

Well as Abby took off so did all the male dachshunds; they jumped out of their section and into hers getting them disqualified as they both came to the line. We picked them up and put their leashes back on.

I put Touché's hot dog costume back on her and we left. I was so proud of my princess.

My grandpa made more ramps for the girls in the house for their backs. One day I was on the couch with both of the girls when my grandparents came in asking if I wanted to run errands with them. I said yes and told both girls we would be right back and we left and told Touché she was in charge and shut the door behind me.

While we were gone Abby jumped off the couch without using the ramp and broke her back in half and started whimpering. I can only imagine for hours and died. I had to call my cousin that day when we got back and had to tell her; her baby passed away. We both cried that day on the phone.

Chapter 24: Rock Solid

Well soon we went back to Texas and this time my mom and I made a move to Plano, Texas. I was here for my middle and high school years.

Soon, my mom meets a guy named Greg. One day my mom invites him over and he meets us at the swimming pool. Well, I am very wary of the men my mom brings in, but I had a very good feeling about him.

We jumped in the pool and started to swimming. When I was swimming I was wearing earrings and one of my earrings fell to the bottom of the pool. He noticed and I touched my ear and told him not to worry about it but he insisted on finding it for me; then he dived under the water and kept searching until he found it. As he gave it back I thanked him and put it back on.

We kept swimming that night for a couple more hours then we said our goodbyes and my mom and I went back home. After a couple years passed my mom and him got back into contact and it took off from there.

Soon it was going so well he proposed to my mom and she said yes, and we were going to have a wedding. We all decided to get a house together and live as one happy family. It was soon time to prepare for the wedding and get things in order; before we all knew it was time for the rehearsal dinner. We all decided we wanted Mexican food to eat and invited family and friends and gave toasts and speeches to the bride and groom.

We all ate and had toasts flowing out like wildfires and then as we were eating everyone thought the toasts were dying down. I was very quiet and then said I would love to make a toast to the bride and groom and everyone turned around. I grabbed the microphone and stood up I started off with Greg.

I said I met Greg at a pool and our first interaction with each other was him finding my earring and I said I thought it was gone one tiny little earring vs. the whole pool. I told him not to worry about it but he dived down and found it for me anyway. And I am so happy that you are going to be a part of the family. Then I shifted to mom and said I love you with all my heart and I can't tell you enough on how much you mean to me. You are my world and without you. I am not me. After that I hugged my mom and we enjoyed the rest of the night.

I just didn't know how bad it would turn out so fast soon a few years passed and it was 2010 and my mom was pregnant with my baby sister, London Bleu Riddell. Her room was painted a baby blue and my aunt came over to paint a tree on her wall. It was an absolutely stunning picture of a tree and a swing.

My mom got some Eiffel tower decorations and her name plastered on her wall with huge letters that my mom got from Hobby Lobby and painted them and hung them on her wall. My room was right next door and teal.

Soon my mom was pregnant again with another baby girl, my second sister, Priscilla Jane Riddell and we were all one big happy family.

London started growing up and I specifically remember this one night it was Greg, the girls and I at the house and we were playing games and mom was out and then later that night I helped Greg put the girls to bed. I then read London a book and then went to my room to lay down and go to bed and everyone was fast asleep when we heard a sound. Greg went to the front door well these two strangers where walking up our steps to our house with my mom clearly intoxicated and her arms wrapped around their necks and they dropped her off and left.

I heard her come in the house and her and Greg arguing that night saying everyone was asleep as she tried to maintain her balance, and then I saw her walking and knocking over picture frames.

I got out of bed and asked Greg if mom was okay, and he said she will be and then I nodded and walked back in my room. Then I hear more talking and then I see my mom try to come into my room. She comes in, stumbles a bit and makes it to the other side of the bed with me; pulls the covers up and falls asleep.

Chapter 25: If I went mad, we must have a cup of tea.

Well, I might have mentioned to you at the very beginning of this book that I have epilepsy. I have to do stuff maybe a little differently from other people. Well while I was living with my family I was put on a medication for them called Keppra.

On November 17th 2016, I was having multiple seizures again. My stepdad was the only one at the house. I was watching TV then, boom, my left hand started to rise and I could feel myself leaning. I screamed for Greg to come; as he rushed in, he saw I was seizing and so he started to move the table so if I fell, I didn't hurt anything or fall off the couch and hurt myself.

He gently laid me on the couch and started calling my mom and then the second phone call was to the paramedics. The paramedics stormed into our house and was setting all their gear down to look at me and make sure I was okay. Then they put me on a gurney and put me in the back of the ambulance.

We rushed off with Greg trying to still get into contact with my mom. As soon as she read it, she met us there at the hospital. I looked at her and smiled.

As soon as I was feeling better, we came home and started back up our little life, but soon things took a heavy turn and the medication I was on made me hallucinate. I was running around the house - most days out of it - and screaming and terrified, stating there are sharks chasing me, there are sharks chasing me, as my mom looked behind me and saw nothing out of the ordinary.

At this stage in my life I was petrified I was hallucinating, seeing stuff that wasn't there, mainly shadows and just freaking out. Soon my mom said come with me and we drove to somewhere and it turned out to be an insane asylum. She turned off the car. We both got out and walked inside and she started to fill out the form. As she wrote I was looking around the place and getting a feel for it. I can say I wanted out.

The person came over to where my mom and I were sitting and said, This is where you'll be. I looked over to where he was pointing and saw a huge spacious cell with the door heavier than ever. I turned back to my mom and pleaded with her, and she looked down at the form one last time and she took me by the hand, gave the paperwork back, and we walked out.

I was furious with her because in my head she was about to lock me up if I went mad, which I can safely say I did for a while. I first wanted my cup of tea.

Chapter 26: Peeps and Runways

As time went on and we started getting things somewhat normal again, my mom figured out we needed to change seizure medications and I felt much better with no hallucinations and was feeling like my normal self again.

My mom decided to go to schooling for cosmetology and found a salon. Paul Mitchel, It was a blast. This is the salon I went to when I had prom and my mom colored and cut my hair.

Well one day we both came, and it was a runway show. I looked at all the pretty models that day getting their hair done and make-up. All of a sudden in one quick motion a guy came over and told my mom that we were going to be short one model and we needed one more to make it complete. My mom turns her head in my direction and I just say, "Me?" And she asked me if I could fill in for the show and that she would do my hair and make-up. I looked around and saw everyone getting theirs done and how beautiful they looked and so I agreed.

She quickly grabbed my hand and sat me down in a chair and spun me around so I was facing the mirror and got everything out of her bag. I saw her get a curling iron, can of hairspray, chopsticks, ribbon and a bag of peeps and started with my hair, sticking colored peeps onto the chopsticks. Then she curled my hair and stuck the chopsticks into my hair and hair sprayed it once done; then stuck the ribbon in.

After that she started working on my make-up and with all different colors, put tiny little dots on my forehead all the way across my cheeks and down my chin, then finished it off with a red lipstick and red false eyelashes and purple tulle going around my neck with a big purple bow.

Then we heard it was time to line up on stage and I took my place and waited until it was my turn to walk down the runway. As I walked down I waved and smiled, went all way down, stopped and turned, posing a few times and then walked back.

I was the last one to go and as I finished the runway closed and we started packing are things back up. Then my mom's friend came up and asked if we wanted to go to dinner. My mom said yes and I went to dinner that night with peeps in my hair and my make-up still on. It was definitely a one-of-a-kind night.

Chapter 27: Help I've Fallen and Can't Get Up!

A couple days later go by and we were hanging out on the couch and my mom and Greg decided to get the house cleaned. Well, we decided to go out for lunch at a restaurant right up the street in walking distance.

We get up and start getting ready to go out for lunch and we all meet in the garage. I look and see my little sister and totally forgot about the little wagon. She was getting to the point where she was getting too heavy to carry. I said hold on I'm going to get her wagon and I'll be right back.

Well I came out of the garage and turned the corner to the tile where the maid was cleaning and I slipped and fell on my wrist. The maid came over to see if I was okay and I said yeah I'm okay and tried to get up and couldn't. Now fear was rushing in because I was on the tile for a good solid few minutes just lying there before I forced myself to get up. I used the wall as a guide to walk and get her wagon so she could ride in it.

I grabbed it and started to move it while feeling an immense amount of pain in my wrist; but I finally drug it out and was back in the garage where I told my mom what happened about my wrist and how much it was starting to hurt. She said it will be fine and so we went on to eat lunch and again I started to talk about the pain I was feeling.

My mom decided to go across the street and get me a wrap for it and she talked about us girls going shopping. I couldn't even hold my hand above my head, let alone my wrist didn't like to be touched.

I was thinking to myself how in the world am I going to try on clothes? Well we went shopping afterwards and we went to all kinds of spots in the mall, and I was trying something on in the dressing room. I couldn't move my arm above my head to take off my shirt to try on my new one I really liked. I started to hold it tightly, well out of the dressing room and Mom was paying for everything. I tried one more time I said, "Mom, please it hurts," and she said well maybe we should look at it. We went to the ER and they took an ultrasound of the wrist and came back and said my wrist was fractured.

I saw where it broke, and they said they could get a brace and I would have to wear it until it healed over again. After the doctor, left mom said, "I'm so sorry; we will get it better, and we will do what it takes." I hugged her and said thank you.

Chapter 28: Ride or Die

My mom always told me while I was with her that she was my "ride or die´- meaning someone is extremely loyal to another person; which was true. I looked to my mother for a lot of things while I was growing up; mainly because that was all I had and all I knew. We grew and leaned more towards each other especially when it was just the two of us living together on our own in our apartment. And let's say those were the days her and I were the tightest out of our relationship.

We went to each other for everything and it was the happiest times in my life and we both knew we both had each other's backs going forward in our little life together. And it has been that way for a long time running until we hit a fork in the road, but I'm getting ahead of myself here.

Chapter 29: Gadgets, gizmos a-plenty

Soon it hit summer and I was so excited because we were going to take a trip to California and our whole family was going to be there and I couldn't wait to see my baby girl again.

We all were packed and ready to take the early-bird flight the next morning so we could arrive there around nine in the morning and see everyone as they showed up later. My aunt was driving with her son and we had to also pick up my cousins from the airport later that afternoon. My aunt got there around eleven o' clock. We got lunch together; we went to Del Taco and brought it back to eat.

Once we were done it was time for my cousins to be picked up so my grandpa went to go pick them up while we waited at the house for them. As soon as they returned they put their suitcases where they were sleeping for that night. The next morning we woke up at 5:30-6 to get up and get ready to drive to Disneyland to be at the gates when they started to open them up.

My grandpa dropped all of us off and then went back home with the dogs. As soon as they opened the gates people gathered and made their way in and we were now running around the park that day and our group separated ways.

My cousins and I ventured off one direction while the rest of the group stuck together, and we met again in the middle of the park. My grandma paid for the resort there at The Grand Californian and with that hotel you could just walk right into the park.

One day while we were there we were watching the parade and suddenly I had to go the restroom so I told everyone where I was going and my sister had to go as well. I took her hand and started walking in that direction then a worker came out and put his hand out to stop so we stopped walking. Then just like that Princess Ariel came out and I freaked out I was so excited to see her. While she walked by us she blew London a kiss and then we looked back and he still had his hand up for us to stop and a mama duck and her ducklings started to pass through.

I remember looking at the restrooms like, okay breathe; and I told London once we go you and I are running to the restrooms. When we finally finished and came back to the group everyone was like what was the hold up and I said Ariel was walking by and then a mama duck and her ducklings were passing by. And yeah, we had a lot fun in California again but soon it was time to go back home to Texas.

Chapter 30: I'm With Shea

I'M WITH SHEA
#StandUpDontStandBy

As we returned home and got settled again, I returned to my high school at Plano West Senior high school to be a junior. It was amazing! I loved all my teachers and was even a cheerleader for my school.

I was on cloud nine but things soon shifted. My junior year I got bullied, text messages rolling in like wild fire. As the day went on it got to the point where I just flipped my phone over and started crying.

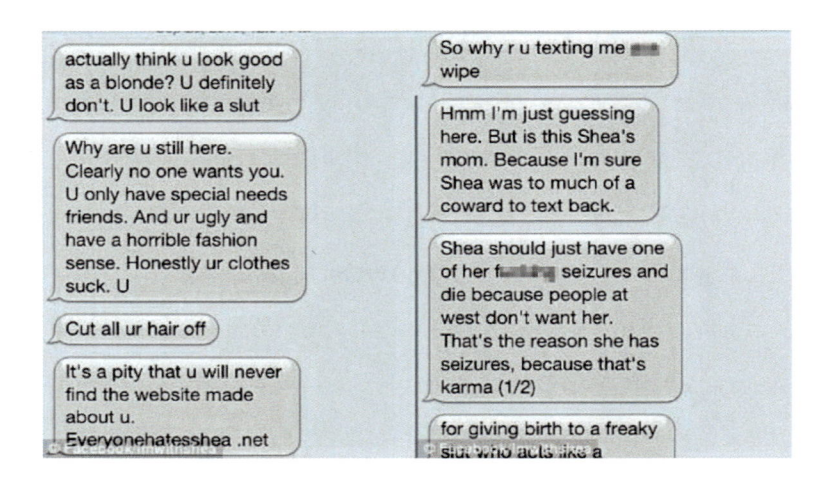

> actually think u look good as a blonde? U definitely don't. U look like a slut
>
> Why are u still here. Clearly no one wants you. U only have special needs friends. And ur ugly and have a horrible fashion sense. Honestly ur clothes suck. U
>
> Cut all ur hair off
>
> It's a pity that u will never find the website made about u. Everyonehatesshea .net

> So why r u texting me ███ wipe
>
> Hmm I'm just guessing here. But is this Shea's mom. Because I'm sure Shea was to much of a coward to text back.
>
> Shea should just have one of her f██████ seizures and die because people at west don't want her. That's the reason she has seizures, because that's karma (1/2)
>
> for giving birth to a freaky slut who acts like a

The bullying started when I was in middle school and increased from there leading into high school and they said I better not be going to West, cause they didn't want me. Well, as this went on I couldn't even function throughout my normal day because I got text messages continuously every day. I couldn't even go up the stairway in my school because a message would roll in saying I see you right now and so every time I walked up the stairs I couldn't walk them without looking to see if someone was watching me before I continued walking up.

And then another message rolled in saying I saw you walking up the stairs. I was terrified looking both ways; I thought my life was over then. I would come home and not talk to anyone; go straight to my room and lay on the floor for hours.

Soon word got out about this girl in Plano, Texas being bullied, and it took off from there. Soon Fox News found out and showed up at our house for an interview and so I was on Fox and that same night I was on the news titled, "High school junior, Shea Shawhan, special needs bullied in Plano, Texas." They wrote a whole article about it.

Once I told my mom about the bullying, my mom made a Facebook page called, "I'm with Shea" and my mom made t-shirts that said "I'm with Shea" in colors neon green, black, and hot pink and one more color (but sorry y'all I can't remember the color), and on the back, they said, "I've got Shea's back, do you?"

The shirts were a hit and then we got orders coming in wanting shirts and all our fan mail piled to our house. I read every letter I received and taped it on my wall making one big "I'm with Shea" wall.

Soon it was summer, and I went to visit my dad and more texts started flooding through. I got depressed again and my dad wasn't the nicest about it. I wasn't myself anymore and it made me sad. I loved hanging out with my dad and we did so much or just hung out, but soon it was time for me to go and I flew back home.

Well the homecoming dance was coming up for my school and I wore my lime green "I'm with Shea" dress. I felt like a princess, so flowy. Then we got to go to a studio and take pictures. I got my hair and make-up done and the photo shoot began.

Well, then on October 13, 2013, the Maverick's basketball team had a scrimmage and found out I was being bullied and they invited me to come watch them. I got to shoot a free throw shot and made it! The crowd was on their feet cheering.

Literally only a couple days after the Maverick's game, Glenn Beck found out about me and on October 13th 2013, I went to Glenn Beck at his studio in Dallas, Texas, and he interviewed me.

My mom and I sat on his couch and got right into the conversation, with what was going on at school. He asked, "Well, Shea what is going on?" I replied with saying just some mean, cruel stuff. I told him, "I'm not that type of person, will never be that type of person to do or think or become one in the first place; but when people say stuff like this, I just kinda think about it for a second. Kinda take a step back and say, "Am I one? No. So why do I care about what people think of me. It's what I think of me or my mom or family think of me, so that should be the most important part; and so I thought about it. I know it's not true, so I'm going to go on with my life and just live a happy life."

We were there for a while before we said our goodbyes and went back home and enjoyed the rest of our day. Then after a couple days went by and we recovered from our drive it was football time. On October 19th, 2013, we went to Waco, Texas, to relax and have fun and watched our favorite football team, the Baylor Bears.

We had a tailgate before the game and had a tent with a covering that said, "I'm With Shea." We ate Frito pies and everything in between. It was such a fun night and we got to see such an amazing game played that night.

Well, yes, someone else heard and on October 26, 2013, my mom and I went to Mela, New York. That was the night I got first class seats and a steak dinner with mashed potatoes yum, and dessert a mountain lava cake. Soon we landed and got checked into our hotel and then went out for the night. Time Square was beautiful and then we saw a street dog stand. That was the first time I had a street dog and especially in New York. New York was amazing. I couldn't believe where I was for a second.

We walked around Time Square all night checking out the night life until we were exhausted and went back to our hotel. We stayed there only for a couple of days before returning home. Then on October 27th, 2013, I had another interview with Mike Huckabee. My mom came with me, and we talked about everything that happened to me at school again.

Then a month passed, and it was November 8, 2013. Our rival school, McKinney High School, had a green out. We went to their school and was welcomed with open arms. It was football night at McKinney High Lions versus Plano West High. As we arrived, I saw a bunch of posters that said, "I'm with Shea" and as I came in I was interviewed and then got pictures with everyone from McKinney students.

I loved every second of that school. And even Selena Gomez heard, and my mom and I were invited to her concert, and I was even put on TIME magazine front cover.

Chapter 31: Graduation

Soon it was that time June 13, 2015, my graduation. We went to my school, and I got my diploma and after that was over, we celebrated and went to Hibachi Grill. My whole family was there and we sat down and ate and had everyone gathered around the tables and we ate dinner. I had a graduation dachshund with a pen to write on it.

My sisters were so small when I graduated, and I wasn't really expecting so many people to arrive for my party, but I guess I'm that loved. Now I was finally graduated from high school and did it feel good.

Chapter 32: Parade of Colors

Soon I had an interview for a job and talked and sat through orientation and filled out a sheet out for them. I was really hoping to land this job because who can say they have worked with Crayola. I hope not a lot at least. Well, I got a call back and I landed it and they said they would love for me to be a part of their team.

This was my first job ever and loved this job. I had my bright yellow highlighter shirt and my pin with my name and my favorite color on it. I even got a pin that said, "Best employee," and I was so proud of myself.

As I was working my mom went back to her old ways again. Greg couldn't take it going back and forth with her, so he filed for divorce and things started to spiral out of control and things went to mayhem.

Chapter 33: Home Sweet Home

My mom and I moved out and found a nice apartment close by so that way we could still be able to see the girls and they could still see their mom and sister.

I still was working at Crayola and enjoying our new little place together. I'll be throwing this in here from goldilocks and the three bears, but "it was just right," especially for only two people living in a home.

Things were not about to get better I quickly realized that in no time at all. Well with my sisters growing up, it was hard. My baby sister Priscilla has asthma which she got from her dad, and I remember we had to wrap a breathing thing around her and put it on her face so that way she could just breathe. It was horrible and I wanted to help her so badly and try to take it away.

On top of that I was becoming a full time parent while my mom was sleeping most hours of the day which meant sometimes I was the one taking care of my sisters; running their baths for them, feeding them dinners, making sure they got up on time when it was time for them to go home and start their school day.

It was mentally and physically exhausting, but I did it because those two little girls are my whole world and I will do all that and more for them and anyone else.

Well here went my mom ... she brought strangers into our house that evening and I remember them talking very loudly and I had to go work the next day so I walked out and saw about roughly if I remember correctly about three men with my mom our apartment, laughing, drinking and talking well I finally had enough because it was so loud and got out of bed and went out my bedroom, saw my mom in the kitchen with these three strangers I bet she didn't even know.

I remember saying to the men, "Get out!" well my mom backed them up saying, "Stay. This is my daughter who should be asleep right now. I yelled at my mom and said I didn't know how low she would stoop. Let me just say it was low.

Well, she got herself a boyfriend, his name was Bryan Alexander.

Chapter 34: Falling into Boxes

Well since my mom got a divorce from Greg, he wanted his ring back that he gave to her. The ring was in storage, so we drove there to find it and give it back to him. Once we parked and went inside, we went to ours and opened it up. Oh my word was that storage a mess. Boxes on top of boxes. Stuff just sitting around and in the open. It was a lot to go through for one small tiny ring, but I knew it was important to Greg.

So we searched and searched and searched, opening boxes one by one. I was soon getting tired because we have now been in the storage for hours looking and looking and nothing showed up. Well as I was looking, I was climbing to try to reach more of the boxes; I slipped, fell down and hit the cement on the floor in there. On top of that, had all the boxes that were piled high get knocked down and fell on top of me.

My mom looked to see if I was okay, and I said, "Yes, just fine," and we continued our search, eventually finding it in my mom's earing holder.

Chapter 35: Kitties R. US

Soon my birthday came around and my aunt, my mom and I went to the pound to look at animals, and I saw this beautiful cat. Now I'm normally not a cat person, but he was beautiful and had the most gorgeous eyes. I instantly knew he was the one I wanted to get.

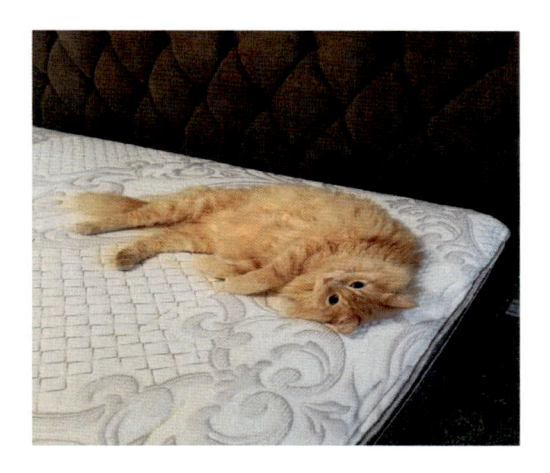

My aunt bought him for me for my birthday present. His name Harley, and I didn't want to leave his side for very long. We brought him to his new home and I loved how I had a new companion to take care of and be by my side every day and trust me.

Cats weren't my thing I tried owning a few. On my last cat I had I accidentally left the door open when I checked the mail and it ran away. That cat's name was Mittens because he had fur covering his paws and so I thought of mittens.

When the girls were over for the weekends, or it was our time to watch them, he was so good with the girls; but hated our furniture and started clawing our recliner, so we had to declaw him.

Chapter 36: Courts in Session

Well soon my mom went away somewhere. I didn't even know where she went, but she left me home alone for days so I was on my own. I made myself dinner, watched TV and played with Harley for days and then my mom said she was coming home.

I wanted the house to be cleaned for her and so I started in the garage. I grabbed my phone and a broom and started sweeping all the leaves out of the garage and back into the street and started organizing the garage as well. Well as I was cleaning and listening to music, I texted my cousin, Logann, on what she was doing for today. She said she was busy and asked what's going on at the house. So I told her I was home by myself and wanted to hang out with her.

She exclaimed she was telling her stepdad, Barry, and he was now on his way over to pick me up. Well I texted my mom saying I was going to hang out with Logann for a bit and she said okay. Soon he arrived in his truck and I didn't know it then, but it turned out much longer than just one day of me staying with them.

I lived there for a while, and it came out a whole blown out thing when my mom reached out to me and my aunt told me not to text her back. So, my mom started messaging my aunt as well saying that I needed to come home.

While I was there I was still working even though I was at her house and I was also going to work with my aunt at her salon called Salon a la Mode and was quite happy again.

Until one day my mom showed up at my work at Crayola and I got a text message from my aunt saying I needed to leave and that she was in the back of the building and that my mom was trying to find me.

Well, I left out the back and entered her car and we went to pick up my cousin and we went home, and my aunt got a temporary restraining order against my mom and she couldn't come near me.

Well, one day some cops showed up at the house and sat me down and talked to me and was saying stuff about my mom and how she was trying to get ahold of me. I told them I just wanted to be with my aunt at her house and it was safe for me here and they said okay, tipped their hat and walked out the door and told my mom.

Well then, my mom brought things to court and my dad then flew out to stay with me throughout that time and everyone was there, me, Shelley, my dad, my cousins, and they even called upon Greg to be there as well.

I was terrified when I was speaking to the judge; he asked me eventually after everyone else what they wanted for me; finally, he asked me what I wanted.

I then looked around the court room at everyone and then finally said I would like to be with my mom, and it just came out.

To be honest I was scared of my mom and so I stayed with her.

And then the judge took my statement into consideration and granted her, and she won, and my dad went back home.

Chapter 37: Saddle Up!

As we were walking out of court and on our way back to Bryan's house (mom's boyfriend), I couldn't help but think about dad and him having to travel back to Tennessee.

Well, we got back to Bryan's house on July 21, 2018, and when I arrived it was quiet, and I saw one of mom's friends there sitting down at the table. And then I heard tiny voices coming from upstairs and everyone told me to crouch down and hide by the table and my two sisters very little started to come to the hall and asked about me and I shot up and London and little baby PJ ran down the stairs and London jumped into my arms and PJ was hugging my leg as she came down for a hug.

Well, my mom said that we were going to see my aunt in White Mound in Sherman, Texas, for a couple of days and we stayed at her house for a week to two. On one night while we were there my aunt took us to go to the rodeo and see all the cowgirls with their horses. They put on the best show, jumping over things and then the real fun began when the bulls started to come up and they tried to throw off the guys riding them.

While I was there, I was wearing heels and while I was walking back and forth a rock got lodged into the bottom of my heel and is still there to this day.

Then when it was over we went back inside and had game night with the rest of the people that were in there. Before it got late, we got up, went to the car and went back home. Soon the two weeks were up and we went back to Bryan's house.

Chapter 38: And the color parade continues

    We have been at Bryan's house now for a while and the girls and I got used to living with him at his house and was pretty comfortable with him. I mean the man had a whole movie theater in his house and the girls and I slept upstairs while him and mom slept downstairs.

    Well, I was also going to my work from his house and Ubering there and back. One night I had to work and I had to work two shifts that night because it was an event night at Crayola which was adult night and my manager asked me if I could stay later since it was an event night, and I said of course.

    I was there working and telling them how to work everything and even had karaoke in the back of the room with people singing. Since I had to work double shifts that night and when things finally started to settle down and we were done, it was one o' clock in the morning. I told my manager I cleaned all the attractions and told my manager goodbye and headed out and ordered my Uber to return to Bryan's house.

    As I was waiting for my Uber to come, I got a call from my mom after working that shift and I answered it. She was crying and she said, "Shea, I left the door open and now I can't find the cat." Well, I just did a double shift and was exhausted and just replied with, "Look for him and I'm on my way back so I can help look."

As soon as I got home, I started joining my mom and her boyfriend by knocking on doors asking if they had seen a cat walk past and they said no I'm sorry and I was crying while walking door to door, each one saying no and breaking my heart just a bit more each time.

Soon my mom's boyfriend found him and he was hiding underneath a bush curled up in a ball and he grabbed him and we took him home.

Chapter 39: Palm Trees, a cool breeze, and a "yes, please"

Well, I had my schedule and I worked only a few days out the week and only worked more when they needed the extra help. And even though I was working a couple nights before, I was called upon to come back and started working right away and worked until my lunch break. My manager was there and told me that my phone has been blowing up and I looked at it and I saw my mom blowing up my phone with text messages saying to call her asap.

I called her back and she answered and she told me, "Shea honey, you need to quit your job. I'm going into rehab and I just booked you a plane ticket to California to live with your grandparents." I was shocked but still managed somehow to say okay and she said when I get home she would be already gone and she hung up the phone. I turned around to my manager and I told her I quit and she asked me why and I told her what my mom told me and I walked out of the breakroom that day devastated. I left Crayola that afternoon and took an Uber to the house to pack a suitcase and then took another Uber to the airport.

Once I got to the airport and went through security and I got to my gate, I texted my grandma I was at my gate. I was still wearing my work uniform while at the airport and didn't have time to change into something more comfortable and it was a 3hr 26 min flight.

When I was on the plane and we were in the air I fell asleep and didn't wake up until we were landing. As we landed I grabbed my phone and turned it on and texted my grandma that I just landed. Then I had to wait until everyone left so I could get up and start my way off the plane and grabbed my minnie backpack and was walking down until I hit the escalators and was coming down then I saw them my grandma and grandpa. I ran to give them hugs and we left the airport.

My grandpa had a gray van at the time and was easy to point out while they asked if I was hungry, I said yes so our first stop, yep, Del Taco. We got food from the drive thru and took it back to the house and as we pulled into the driveway the dogs were barking and wagging their tails looking out the window. I felt back at home again all of them running down the ramp and going to the door and running back and forth to each door seeing which door we would come in.

As we entered the house the dogs jumped and sat still while we ate as they stared at us.

I stayed in the room I had as a little girl, everything in the exact same place and not touched or moved and everything was like when I was a little girl again.

I opened my closet door and saw my pink sparkly princess skirt I had for dance and tried it on, and it couldn't go past my ankles, lol.

And soon I was settled back in and living my best life with my grandparents and playing with my baby girl (dog) again, and of course I had my best friend back, my grandpa.

Chapter 40: Trouble in Paradise

Well, California has earthquakes and had an earthquake one night and so I slept straight through it. One day my grandma tried waking me up and nothing happened and I didn't budge. Turned out I had a couple of seizures there on the couch, so my grandma called my mom cause she was worried about me.

My mom got a plane ticket and took a break from her rehab to come see me and she stayed with me for a couple of days then when she saw I was feeling better had to go back because she couldn't stay. The rehab wouldn't let her stay gone long.

When she was gone, I was feeling a bit like myself again but had a huge headache but it went away in a couple weeks. A couple of months went by and then one night I was asleep until the next morning when my grandma woke up and saw Touché. She was still and shaking; she ran upstairs and shook my bed. I woke up and she said, "Touché." That's all she had to say. I jumped out of bed and rushed downstairs I turned the corner and saw her there still and shaking with her biting her tongue.

I asked what is happening; she responded with she's having a seizure. I picked her up, held her in my arms and sat on the couch until she was done. Her tongue was bleeding, and I was bawling crying saying I was the only one supposed to have them.

I petted her over and over, so she knew I was still there with her; then after a couple of more minutes, it was over. After that I put her down on the carpet. She was off balance and wobbly.

I was a mess all day having her in my line of sight. I didn't feel right with her on the floor, so I picked her back up and put her on the arm of the couch and she curled in a ball and I put a blanket on top of her and put my arm around her.

Chapter 41: Rehab for One

That night I asked my grandpa if he could play a game of Trouble with me. While we were in the middle of our game my grandma got a call from my mom and she had something to tell me. We stopped playing and she handed me the phone.

My mom was on the call and she asked me on how I would feel if I lived with her in Florida. I sat up and was really excited and I said I would love too, and then that was the last night with my grandparents.

The next morning, I was on my flight. I was excited to see my mom again. The flight was 4hrs and 52 minutes. I slept for half of it. When we landed, I texted my mom and we went to baggage claim, grabbed my bags and we went home. When we got to the house our shit-tzu, Teddy, was there bouncing up and down.

Once in and settled, my mom mentioned to me that she had to go to her meeting for her rehab and said she was leaving in a couple of minutes. While my mom was gone, I watched TV with Teddy and had dinner.

Chapter 42: This beauty is a beast.

While in Florida I was on a drive with my mom and on our way to our destination I looked over and saw this kickboxing place and I told my mom about it. She signed me up and I started the next day. I walked in and talked to the trainers and they signed me up for a membership and then grabbed me some boxing gloves and set me up with a bag and it was an hour class.

They stayed with me for my first day and then they had a bootcamp and I paid for it and it was at the beach. And oh boy it was a lot, when we weren't doing bootcamps we were in the studio and we were on our regular schedule and sometimes they would pair us up.

While at the studio I started to hit hard and one day when I came in they mentioned that they had the kickboxer of the month and I was looking around seeing who it is and I drank my drink I had and in mid-sip, they mentioned my name and I spit it back out and pointed to me.

They said "You are a beauty but when you hit the mat you're a beast."

I was so happy and took a picture of the board and walked back home after class and as soon as I walked in, I told my mom, and she was so proud of me.

I boxed there for months and loved that studio and thought of everyone in there as my family or I called it (my fit fam).

Chapter 43: Salon A la Mode

On Tuesday May 5th, 2020, four years ago a booking photo provided by the Dallas county sheriff's office shows my aunt (Shelley Luther). My aunt was booked on Tuesday after the state district judge sentenced my aunt to a week in jail because she refused to close her north Dallas business, her hair salon; Salon a' la Mode, due to the coronavirus and was fined $7,000 dollars for criminal and civil contempt.

The judge found out that she was still running her salon in violation of the governor's order and violation of the restraining order that my aunt had ripped up. The judge said he would consider not giving my aunt any jail time if she admitted that she was wrong and came out saying she was selfish and that she should apologize to the elected officials.

My aunt responded with this, "I have to disagree with you, sir, when you say that I'm selfish because feeding my kids is not selfish. I got hairstylists that are going hungry because they'd rather feed their kids. So sir, if you think the law is more important than kids getting fed, then please go ahead with your decision but I'm not going to shut down the salon."

And my aunt was sentenced to each day her salon was open and she was in the Dallas County jail with a $500 dollar fine for each day it was open.

But as her niece I will stand by her, and I can say my aunt made a decision and it was hers alone and it was the right one to make. She needed to feed her husband, her two daughters and her stepson. She needed to feed her family.

Chapter 44: The day Touché found her wings!

I had now been with my mom for a couple of months and enjoying being her roommate while living here in Florida. It was January 24th 2021, and we needed groceries. Our fridge was looking pretty sad and empty, so I told my mom we needed to go shopping today.

We went to the grocery store (Target), grabbed our cart and we barely had anything in our cart - maybe two to four items. I remember going down the aisle for something with my mom and then got a phone call.

I looked down and I saw it was my grandma. I answered the phone happy as could be then I heard from the other end, "Shea honey, are you sitting down?" I replied no and she said well you might want to; and she said, "Shea-Shea, Touché passed away today."

My whole world turned upside down and I collapsed on the aisle floor and cried my eyes out. I asked my grandma what happened to her. Well she had to rush her to the vet cause her lipoma had popped and blood rushed to her stomach but the vets said they couldn't do much and put her to sleep so she didn't have to live in pain.

I eventually got up and I told my mom and she looked at me with tears in her eyes and said, "Forget the groceries," left the cart and we went back to the car and drove home. My mom ordered groceries at the house and were delivered so we now had food.

When Touché died I became obsessed with dachshunds to this day.

Before I knew it I was crying every night because I lost my best friend, then cried myself to sleep, as I woke up I saw my mom standing in the living room and I saw a chocolate-shaped dachshund. I never ever ate that chocolate dachshund as I put it on my night stand in my room.

Chapter 45: Let's just have one more seizure, shall we?

Soon January 6, 2022, hit and at this time I was twenty-five years old. I was at the house with Teddy and on the couch that night and my mom was at her NA meeting. Before she left she asked if I'll be okay; I said yes and she told me I'm a phone call away just in case.

She left, and not too long after she shut the door, maybe five to ten minutes after she shut the door, and she was probably already on the road to her meeting, a rush came over me and my heartbeat got heavier and my left hand started to go up and shaking in the air and I started to fall off the couch.

Well, Teddy saw this and immediately went into action; he got up from laying down and came onto my chest and layed his head down staying there for a while. Then he got up and started to tug on my hair and by doing that got me off the couch and onto the carpet.

From there I got enough strength to try to do something and awkwardly walked to our front door to open it. As soon as it was opened, I walked over to the neighbor's house and started banging on their door for help. No one answered the door, so I knocked again. Someone answered the door and I said I need help.

Not long after he let me in, I saw he was having a party while the room was blurry I felt bad for crashing it but then Boom! I was on his living room floor seizing. They noticed I was wearing my epilepsy necklace and said, "Time it" and someone else called the paramedics to come.

When I left my house, I left the front door open and Teddy got out of the house, but I was already gone by then. They put me in the gurney and in the back of the ambulance and rushed off while teddy was running around the complex.

Once I was in my room and they put an IV in my arm, then I see my mom, what it looked like at least. I look at her and immediately started to cry, but I was a little out of it at the same time.

I got a little bit better and suddenly I screamed, "Teddy," and my mom reassured me he was okay and that our apartment manager grabbed him and is at home now. I felt at ease again and when they cleared me to come home and when I got back home it felt good to see his little face again. It especially felt good being back home from being in that bed in the hospital even if was only for a few hours.

I think not too long after my mom had another NA meeting and right after that her AA meeting, and this time I came with her. When we arrived at her meeting there were a group of people and before the meeting took place and as we sat down they went straight into it and started the meeting everyone there including my mom said their name and I'm an addict and then it got to me I said, "hi my name is Shea and I'm a supporter."

Everyone snapped their fingers and once everyone had a turn they went to it with the twelve steps. The head of the group told someone to read the steps out loud:

Step one: we admitted we were powerless over our addiction and that our lives had become unmanageable.

Step two: believing that a higher power (in whatever form) can help.

Step three: Deciding to turn control over to the higher power.

Step four: taking a personal inventory.

Step five: we admitted to God, to ourselves and to another human being the exact nature of our wrongs.

Step six: we were entirely ready to have God remove all these defects of character.

Step seven: we humbly asked Him to remove our shortcomings.

Step eight: we made a list of all persons we had harmed and become willing to make amends to them all.

Step nine: we made direct amends to such people wherever possible, except when to do so would injure them or others.

Step ten: we continued to take personal inventory and when we were wrong promptly admitted it.

Step eleven: we sought through prayer and meditation to improve our conscious contact with God as we understand Him, praying only for knowledge of His will for us and the power to carry that out; and finally,

Step twelve: having had a spiritual awakening as a result of these steps, we tried to carry this message to addicts, and to practice these principles in all our affairs.

As she finished reading and as she looked up the person teaching said thank you and asked if anyone would like to share. As only a few people shared, they soon closed the meeting with a serenity prayer and said, "God, grant me the serenity to accept the things I cannot change, the courage to change the things I can and the wisdom to know the difference."

My mom got key tags for how long she stayed sober for every one they said, "Clean and serene for nine months" and so on; each one a different color tag.

I was very proud of her and what she accomplished.

Chapter 46: Bruised but not Broken.

A few days passed and one night I felt stuck, and I started to slowly start getting depressed and wanted something else for me but didn't know what.

Then one day my mom's friend came over and her and my mom went to her bathroom and got ready to go out while Teddy and I were on the couch watching TV.

Once they were done my mom came back out with a sparkly dress with her heels on and she said, "Okay babe, we are gone. We will be back later and I looked at her and said, "Take your time and have fun." After she left and locked the door, I looked at Teddy and said it looks like it's just you and me tonight, as he tilted his head to the left and that night.

I made myself and Teddy's dinner and then finished watching TV all night. Soon I looked over at the time and saw it was midnight and grabbed Teddy and headed to my room and put him on my bed and we both laid down. I eventually fell asleep, but two hours later got woken up from Teddy barking.

As he continued I thought I should check it out and sat up in bed and saw the door handle turning like someone was trying to come in from the outside.

I got out of bed and started walking and started walking towards the door as the door opened and I saw my mom and her friend walk in the door and they looked drunk and I confronted them and said, "Where have y'all been? Do you know what time it is?"

It is now two-thirty in the morning and my mom looked up at me with what seemed to be pure hatred at the moment and responded with, "I'm grown. I can do whatever I want." I responded with, "Okay but a grown up also knows when to be a grown up and have some common sense."

And really quick after that it felt like I blinked my eyes and she shifted gears all of a sudden calling me all kinds of names I wont go through all but one was slut. Then she ran over to where I was and grabbed my hair and yanked it down ; and then put my face into a wall. Then I was in a corner and she started scratching my face over and over I told her to please stop.

As soon as I heard myself, I'm now screaming it while she was in my face and she told me to be quiet because the neighbors could hear me. I told her that I didn't care and that she really needed to get out of my face. She didn't and finally I had enough courage and I gave her one more chance to back away and that she just needed to go to bed, screaming it repeatedly for her to listen; but she kept getting in my face.

So the next thing that happened was I front kicked her - yes I front kicked my own mom - she went flying back into her own room and landed. I felt so bad I started walking towards her because half of me wanted to make sure she was okay, but the other half wanted to see what she had done to my face.

All of this is happening while her friend is standing there. I immediately get up and rushed to the restroom to see what she had done to my face and I saw scratches all over my cheeks from her nails. After a while I come out of the bathroom and she got back in my face again and said that I'm not her daughter anymore and that she only had two daughters now and she yelled in my face, "You're gone!"

She went into the living room and I saw a syringe needle on the table and she picked it up and I saw it was filled with something but didn't know what .

Then I started screaming at the top of my lungs multiple times and saying please no then right in front of me she stuck the needle in her arm. As I started to cry and then continued arguing until maybe three in the morning, finally getting her to finally go to sleep that night.

But she came back in my room and threw everything out of my closet and she said I need to call my father cause she was done with me. I told her to calm down and just sleep but she insisted so I grabbed my phone and started dialing knowing he wasn't going to answer.

How I knew? that um it was 3:00 in the morning! Well then I got his voicemail. I hung up and told her with my knees to my chest shaking and said he didn't answer, and she replied with, "Let me guess, he didn't answer; and do you know why, cause he doesn't love you."

And let me tell you, that hit deep and hurt me. I started shaking uncontrollably now and turning my head back and forth saying no that's not true. Now it felt like a waterfall streaming down my face and I finally let the words out and said just please go to sleep.

She then grabbed Teddy out of my hands and slammed my door shut and went into her room. I rolled over and cried myself to sleep that night and before I knew it my eyelids fell and I fell asleep.

By the next morning I woke up and my mom was still asleep and decided to write her a note and that read, "Good morning. I'm at boxing. I will be back soon." Grabbed my water bottle and grabbed my keys and headed out and locked the door behind me.

As I walked into class I was quiet and just really wanted to punch something. I could barely get through it with tears still in my eyes and still not willing to say anything. Soon class came to a close and I started walking back home. As I was walking up our stairs I finally got to our front door where our mat said, "Welcome to the birds nest."

I took a breath and put my hand on the doorknob let's say a good ten minutes then opened the door and saw the TV playing with Teddy and my mom crying on the couch. I didn't know why but I wasn't angry anymore and saw her tears.

As she looked at me and she said she hurt me and she was sorry and look what I did to you. Then I sat on the couch and said its okay while I gave her a hug.

But I was frustrated and didn't quite understand how this happened so fast the way it did.

Chapter 47: Where The Green Grass Grows

Later, I took Teddy out to use the restroom and I got a phone call from my dad returning from the night before when I had called him. I answered the phone and we talked for a while and he asked me is everything okay over there and I said yes they are and we talked about our days for a while and we exclaimed how much we loved one another.

Then hung up the phone and I started to cry again before heading back up to the apartment again and taking off Teddy's leash but as soon as we were back and inside the house again my mom told me that she thinks I should go see my dad for a while.

Well if I'm being honest here I thought she completely gave up on me all at once. I said okay.

I arrived in Tennessee in August of 2022 and once we finally landed and went to baggage claim, I saw him standing there waiting for me. I ran into his arms like I was a little girl again and on the way home I saw all of the green grass surrounding everything and looking how everything was a vivid green and I whispered to myself, "I'm in the state now where the green grass grows."

Chapter 48: Love is an open door

Soon being with dad and now living there it was summer and the girls were coming out to Florida to be with my mom, and I wanted to see the girls, so I asked my dad and he agreed.

I was excited. I hadn't seen them in a long time and was very happy that they were coming. Well, my mom already brought me to the house, and I was waiting at the house with Mr. Bear (Teddy) while my mom went to go pick up the littles from the airport and I tidied up the house, so it didn't look like a tornado just went through our living room.

After I was done cleaning I sat back down on the couch, turned on the TV. Teddy jumped up and went behind my neck and laid down. After a few hours went by he jumped down and went to the window and looked out and saw mom coming back home with the littles.

As I see the girls rolling their suitcases to the door, Teddy runs outside to say hi then he ran back in when everyone came in. We arranged who was sleeping with whom: priscilla with mom and London with me.

After a while it wouldn't be like that. Soon after spending a couple days there we were hitting the middle of summer. Mom had to go back to work and I had the girls by myself that morning to afternoon so I came up with a plan that we would go swimming later.

We were having fun watching The Voice on TV and then something happened and I snap. It was all so fast and to be honest I don't remember how it got there so quick.

I think London and I had a discussion; she gets up out of the bean bag chair and makes her way to the table where she is close to the hallway. Something triggered inside of me and I throw the remote and it goes by her. Now I love my sister and never hurt her so when I threw it she starts crying and going into mom's room and takes her iPad and locks the door behind her.

Then I look at PJ (Priscilla) and she has tears welled up in her eyes and so I sit down with her and I say I'm sorry PJ, and I said I'll talk to London. But first we have to take Teddy to go potty.

I put the leash on him and both of us went downstairs; once he was done, we went back up the stairs I opened the door took off his leash and he jumped back on the couch and he spread out like a mat putting his head between his front two paws.

I told Prisicilla where I was if she needed me. I looked into that hallway and saw every flashback possible. I was terrified of that hallway, but my sister was in there and I needed to talk to her so I went one foot in front of the other until I reached the door.

Oh my word, my head was spinning and everything in my body said to run; but instead, I knocked and said London please let me in. She got up and unlocked the door. I walked in leaving the door open and I saw her laying in bed and on her iPad with her friends on the other end. I told her to please put it away, because I wanted to talk to her for a second. She looked at me and put it away.

I sat down on the bed, and I started talking and said, "Londie I'm sorry, I'm just not myself right now and I'm sorry for getting mad or whatever I was feeling and bringing you into it. This hallway is just not my favorite right now." Then she asked what happened and I said I can't tell you right now, but then asked if she wanted to swim and she lit up and I said okay.

First finish your call with your friends, and she said, "Shea, why did you leave the door open? And I replied, "Because love is an open door."

That night we swam until seven o' clock.

Chapter 49: Did Someone order an ice cream?

One night we decided to have family game night on my sisters' Nintendo switch as a family, which was mom, her boyfriend and I and we sat down and started playing and we were having a lot of fun for most of the game.

Soon my mom and my sisters got up and went into the kitchen and grabbed an ice cream sandwich and as they got up my mom grabs the ice cream and hands them out to the girls and I say I would like one as well since she was right there.

Then her boyfriend asked me a question and I had my head turned to respond to him and my mom grabs an ice cream sandwich and softball winds and throws it hard and it hits the side of my head. My mom doesn't throw easy, remember college softball player. I took the ice cream and rubbed the side of my head and we continued to play while we ate our ice cream.

We played all night until it was time for sleep for the night but, before I went to my bedroom I went to the restroom, and I noticed I started my period and realized I didn't have any hygiene products.

So I left the restroom and saw that my mom's door was shut so I knocked and she opened it and I asked her if I could borrow one of her tampons and she went into her bathroom and grabbed a box of them came back to the door and threw them at me and then slamming her door shut again and I heard her saying, "I'm going to be happy when she lives with her father.

I was heartbroken because I was back to feeling like she didn't want me around anymore. After going back to the restroom and finishing up I came back out and went into my room and went under my covers and my sister and I watched TV for awhile before she wanted to play with my hair until she got tired and went to sleep for the night.

I rolled over and cried myself to sleep once more.

Chapter 50: Ooh Rah!

After a couple of months went by and now, I'm back in Tennessee and we hear that my cousin is graduating from the marines. We went to see him in South Carolina (Paris Island) to watch him graduate.

The drive out was long but exciting and I couldn't wait to stretch my legs again. Soon we arrived and we got out of the car and we went inside a building and walked around. It was really cool. It was all about the marines.

Soon we took a ride and they talked about everything around; it was amazing learning about everything and learning about my daddy's branch.

But soon it was time to meet everyone. We had lunch then got ready for my cousin's graduation. We walked there and sat down on the bleachers. There was a little time before they came out so everyone talked for a bit then it officially began.

Every young marine lined up in rows and started marching down the line and then separated into three big groups faced forward with their hands behind their backs still as a rock and then they started to move and I got to see his position in line and soon it was over.

They shook their hands after announcing their names and then families could come down and give their congrats as everyone started piling in to get photos and hugs. Soon it was time to pack up and go back home.

I gave my cousin a hug goodbye and we all went to our cars it was another peaceful ride back to Tennessee with a lot of stops in between and then home.

Chapter 51: Faith, Trust and Pixie Dust

Well, then a couple of months go by and April 4th, 2023, hits and that is the day I was clueless and trying to pin point answers to what I was reading. My aunt had a brain aneurysm and hemorrhage. I read everything my uncle posted that afternoon. I immediately lost it and I cried for hours on top of hours wondering if she was going to be okay.

My aunt was in a coma and was in the ICU room. I was tearing myself down on how useless I am if I couldn't fly down to hold her hand and let her know her Shea-Shea was there with her. I felt like I was on a sinking boat and I just wanted to get off but what really hurt was no one told me what was happening or anything at all.

All I had were the posts to go by day by day with some being good stuff to then saying she wasn't going to make it, but I know my aunt and she is one hell of a fighter. Then the doctors told my uncle to be prepared because she wasn't going to make it because of all the blood in her cranial cavity.

That she had suffered an aneurysm near there but they said that they weren't equipped enough to save my aunt's life that night and she was lucky enough to just live to make it to the hospital and that there was no hope for my aunt with doctors looking defeated.

That night they transferred my aunt to a different hospital, and they said there were better equipped for something like this but that she might not make it there and that the artery was still leaking into my aunt's skull. My aunt got transferred to another hospital in a bus to Medical City Plano.

Once arrived they wanted to put my aunt to undergo a craniotomy and my uncle thought she wouldn't make it if they did that, so the doctor reached out to Shelley, grabbed her skin by the front of her armpit and twisted and my aunt sat straight up in the bed.

She looked at the doctor and said, "Stop."

They immediately rushed to get an external ventricular drain (EVD); they took her to Neuro ICU and she was unconscious and the neuro surgeon was on call to perform surgery to put the EVD in my aunt's brain; but there was so much blood in the area the scans were unable to show what was happening.

While one of the doctors gave my uncle a stack of paperwork to sign and exclaimed once more that the type of aneurysm and hemorrhaging she was suffering from usually killed the patient before making it to the hospital and that most, if they make it to the ER, don't make it off the operating table. They also mentioned she would need to be ventilated.

When I read that I freaked out because that was when I knew it was real. The doctors were now going to attempt and perform a endovascular coiling which is a form of endovascular embolization to block blood flow into her aneurysm. They did this using a catheter inserted to an artery in her groin.

Unfortunately, the doctors were unable to fix the blood vessel and said her aneurysm is called a saccular aneurysm and said the coil wouldn't help and that they had to turn it over to someone else in the stroke institute.

The doctor said that my aunt wouldn't last another surgery right then and there if they did another surgery so she rested and then on Friday they went back to surgery. They told my uncle to let all family members know.

My aunt was in the hospital for twenty-three days then they could finally let her go home.

You see, next to my favorite Disney princess Ariel, I really like Tinkerbell and that day I had to have some faith, trust and pixie dust.

Chapter 52: Get your booty and shine your doubloons, this is gonna to be one tough sea.

Well, you better get your booty and shine your doubloons, this is gonna be one tough sea. I think I mentioned that I really loved Teddy; he's adorable.

Well one day I was outside on our porch in our rocking chair we have and I was rocking away enjoying being outside when I geta pop-up from my mom on my phone and I clicked on it and there it showed Teddy with no eye and stitches covering where his left eye had been and I looked at his photo and I was mad; let me tell you why I was so mad: because my mom didn't reach out to me and tell me.

Now Touché will always have the majority and my whole heart. She was mine and I do consider her mine to this day, but I can't deny Teddy Bear. He helped me with my broken heart and I love him dearly. Then I talk to my mom after not speaking for a couple of days. I immediately asked about Teddy and how he was healing from surgery and how did his eye even pop out of his socket. My mom replied with he is healing quite well and that when she woke up it was already out of socket, and she didn't know what happened.

My mom said don't worry honey because now he is a pirate which at the time to me was not funny or amusing in any way. Now I love this dog I mean he is only three years old and went into surgery. I could not believe the first thing out of her mouth was about his surgery. No "hi honey or how was your day or how have you've been lately" - it was boom! Here you go and I could not fathom, and I felt like I was losing one more dog.

If that happened my heart could not take it and I stayed outside for a while. I got up after awhile and went in the house still upset and my dad could tell something was bothering me and I replied without him saying a word, "eddy had surgery and he lost his left eye and now he has stitches replacing it," and we sat down and talked about it for some time. So, I guess a yo ho yo ho and a Teddy we go.

Chapter 53: Fins Up

    It was May 2, 2024, and we took a flight out to Orlando, Florida, for my sister's cheer competition. It was located at Walt Disney World. We were staying for five days at the hotel. I was really nervous in going to Florida again. Why? It is the state where my mom lives, but I tried to push all of that aside for the time being.

    We grabbed our suitcases and were off to the airport. Well once we landed, we left the plane and made our way to the baggage claim to fetch our luggage and then got a rental and made our way to the hotel. Once we got settled in for the night we hung out at the hotel.

    We were going to be busy for Disney it was rides galore when we went to the parks early the next morning and it was amazing. We stayed that day until late evening and then drove back to the hotel and chilled out again for the night. Then it was time for bed, and everyone crashed. The next day my sister had practice and while she was practicing, we were waiting for her then we went back to the hotel, and we hung out and ate snacks- yumm - then we watched TV.

Chapter 54: Halos glowing tonight

On Friday May 17th, 2024, I started to pack and fly to Dallas, Texas, to be with my family and after the plane landed, I texted my mom and I got picked up in baggage claim by her and her boyfriend. As soon as I grabbed my bag, we ordered a rental and went to my aunt and uncle's house in Sherman, Texas.

When I arrived, there was a few people already there: my grandma and my aunt and uncle and her son. We hung out for awhile before we played games (Mexican Train), watched baseball and played a game called Bean Boozled. It was awesome, but it doesn't taste the best. Soon it was three o' clock and we went to go pick up my sisters from school. We tried to surprise them.

Once we picked them up we returned home and we started to play again and laughed that night. Well then on Sunday May 19th 2024, we went to a Texas Ranger vs Anaheim Angels baseball game. The game was a blast and we had a suite by first base side for food. We had chicken tenders, popcorn, mini hot dogs, mac & cheese, candy and drinks (Dr Peppers and bottled waters).

The game was starting soon and it was time to play ball. It started off really well but very slow with 0-0 for four innings straight until the Rangers scored in the top of the fourth, and it was 1-0. But soon, all of a sudden, the game shifted, and the Angels won the game; and if I'm being honest, I don't remember the score that night.

I was just having fun with my family.

Chapter 55: Back in the sunshine state

Here I am again back in Florida (aka) the sunshine state. I told myself I would never go back but here I am. I wanted to go for my sisters; I hadn't seen them in what seemed like forever, well on June 29, 2024, I left for Florida and went on the plane. Three weeks prior I was volunteering in Knoxville and tweaked my back and still went on the plane. Once it hit turbulence I winced in pain a bit.

When I landed, I got off the plane and down to baggage claim and saw the girls and they ran to me. I gently said, "Slow because of my back," and hugged them and grabbed my bag and we went to the house.

Once we arrived at the house I walked in and saw my mom and she gave me a hug and I said I hurt my back and she felt bad but, that would only last so long before stuff became undone. We went to bed that night with Teddy and his one eye.

The next morning we had to get up early for Disney. We packed in the car and we were on our way; of course had to stop for bathroom breaks along the way. Once we got there we pulled into Pop Century and settled into the hotel and went to the parks right away.

My back was killing me walking around and one day we were in line for a ride and I got to see my mom's (special side). I was standing in line which by the way was packed and she told me to move out of her way. I started to move and in pain at the same time and was very sad but I cannot for the life of me tell her, "please be nice to me." For me it's like somehow I deserve it. But I didn't do anything to her; it's just how I feel and I take it.

One night at our hotel she decided to put a TENS machine on my back trying to find where it hurt with the highest setting, and it hit the spot. I screamed out in pain and screamed, "Take it off!" Soon our Disney days were over after spending five days there and we headed back home.

For the rest of my time there, we hung out at the house and still in pain. My mom's boyfriend asked what I could do to ease the pain; and I could hear from her room, "She's fine" and I said it's okay and went into my little sister's room for the night.

All I really want is a relationship with her, but I'm feeling I will never have that relationship with my mother like I really want. And that really hurts because after everything that's happened ironically, I still want that relationship, but it feels like it comes with a cost.

Epilogue

I would like to dedicate the last chapter of this book to my Tennessee family who have been there for me through thick and thin. I know I will still be trying to stay afloat, pretending all is okay (despite what happened in Florida). But I will say I have come a long way from the girl I once knew.

I may still be a little quiet, but I am slowly coming out of my shell and opening up. Its just slow and taking a lot longer than I would like it.

My father

My Father is my true rock. I am stuck to him like glue and now that I have him for all time, versus when he couldn't be there, I am so thankful I have him now.

I just hope he knows how much he is loved by me, and I hope he also knows no matter what, he will always have my love and that will never change. I look up to you constantly and I can say that you are forever going to be a hero in my eyes.

My step-mom

I may not speak a lot of my emotions to you or just talk to you about a lot of stuff going on inside of me, but I want to tell you how much I value, love and cherish you. I cannot imagine having my life without you in it; you are my glue to put all my pieces back in order.

It may not be as perfect as before, but that's okay and I know for a fact that without you, I would be a total wreck. You push me and drive me to heights I didn't know I could reach. So here I am with all of my heart saying thank you.

I love you so much that sometimes in conversations I start crying out of nowhere, crazy right! I hope you know when I start crying out of nowhere it's because I have so much love for you that sometimes it comes in one big tidal wave crashing down and it tears me apart because I want to let you know how special you are to me.

My sister Trinity

My sister is everything to me and with her cheer and everything to go along with that. I hope she knows I am her biggest cheerleader. From watching my little sister grow up to watching you become this young lady, let me just say I'm in awe. I will always be here for you, and I will always love you.

My brother Sam

You are my playmate in my life, someone who I can always have to sit down with and share a laugh with.

I love you to the moon and back. I want you to know how much your big sister loves you and nothing can take that away.